Jonathan Dunne

SEVEN BRIEF LESSONS ON LANGUAGE

Published in 2023 by
SMALL STATIONS PRESS
20 Dimitar Manov Street, 1408 Sofia, Bulgaria
You can order books and contact the publisher at
www.smallstations.com

Bible quotations contained herein are from the New Revised Standard Version, Anglicized Edition, copyright © The Division of Christian Education of the National Council of the Churches of Christ in the United States of America 1989, 1995

The cover photograph by Ivelina Berova shows an icon of St Nicholas in the Church of Sts Peter and Paul in the village of Velinovo, near Tran (west Bulgaria). For more information on this photographer's work, please visit her website, www. ivelinaberova.com

The font used in this book is Kometa by Kiril Zlatkov

ISBN 978-954-384-129-5

Jonathan
Dunne

SEVEN
BRIEF
LESSONS
ON LANGUAGE

Small
Stations
Press

*For the background to this book, please see the
series of articles 'Word in Language (0)-(24)'
on the website www.stonesofithaca.com*

In him who sees must be found something of what is seen.

Dumitru Staniloae, *Orthodox Spirituality*,
tr. Jerome Newville and Otilia Kloos (2002)

CONTENTS

FIRST LESSON

The Alphabet

In the spiritual life, we see that the pleasures of this world are finite. If we indulge them without control, we find that they lead to a feeling of emptiness, of dissatisfaction. They lead nowhere, in effect, except for a spiralling downwards centred on the demands of the ego. It is only when we turn outwards and embrace the value of the other that our life begins to take off. There are three stages to this spiritual journey. The first is the acquisition of the virtues to replace the indulgence of the passions. The second is to begin to see God in the world around us. The third is contemplation of God, a stage reached only by the spiritually advanced.

I remember the first time I saw a face in a rock. I was very struck by this. I had been looking at rocks for many years, but I had never noticed anything unusual about them. The world for me was two-dimensional, a place that I could lie down in, or take from, but certainly not one that had its own existence apart from me. It was mine to look at, like a picture. This is a form of spiritual blindness. When we are born, we are physically blind for a few days or weeks. Once we gain our sight and begin to discern the world around us, we think that is it, we are no longer blind and we can see. But we do not realize that there is a second kind of blindness, spiritual blindness, that prevents us from seeing the needs of the other, the existence in the world of other realities, realities that reflect the presence and design of God. The Greeks call these other realities 'logoi' – little words. Not the Word himself, but representations, fragments of him.

When I first saw a face in the rock, I was starting to see these 'logoi'. This coincided, as it had to, with my starting to go to church, to lead a spiritual life. Just as Christ opens the eyes of the man born blind in John 9, so he does this for us, when we believe in him. This doesn't happen suddenly, there's no bright light (at least, not normally), it happens gradually, but our eyes begin to be opened. We discern faces in the rock, faces in flowers, faces in water. The world begins to reveal itself to us as it really is (and not as a source of pleasure and profit, which is how we tend to view it in society).

And just as these 'logoi' exist in the natural world, so they exist in language. Words have a deeper meaning, a meaning that is hidden from us until we begin to apply the poultice of the sacraments, to participate in the spiritual life, to believe in God. Once we do this, the veil is taken from our eyes and we discern something that was right in front of us, but that we hadn't seen. I would like to give an example with the alphabet.

The Latin alphabet as it is used in English comprises twenty-six letters. We don't think about these letters very much – their shape, their order in the alphabet – we just learn to trace their form, we learn what sound they represent, and that way we can take part in communication with others. We can read their thoughts and transmit our thoughts to them even when they are not in the same room by writing them down. But that is pretty much as far as the letters go. We don't think much more about them, as we don't think much more about the field or beach we leave behind, their existence when we are no longer there.

Language, speech, comprises three elements. Without these elements, you cannot speak. The first of them is **breath**. Obviously, it is impossible to speak if you are not breathing, because then you would be dead.

Breath in language is represented by the letter *h*. This little letter, which is not even pronounced in some languages and is sometimes dropped colloquially, is the basis of all speech. Breathe out as if you wanted to polish your glasses and make the sound represented by this letter. You will feel a little warmth in the palm of your hand. There is no voice as yet, only breath. Breath is not a word as such, it doesn't convey any information except to show that we are alive.

If we want to make a word, we must now add voice to breath and form the vowels. There are five vowels, but they are not pronounced in the mouth in the same order as they are included in the alphabet. In alphabetical order, the vowels are *a, e, i, o* and *u*. But the order in which they are pronounced from the back of the mouth (where language originates) to the front is the following: *u, o, a, e* and *i*. If *h* represents breath, the vowels represent water. Hold a vowel sound for long enough, and water will collect in your mouth, just as when you're at the doctor's and the doctor wants to look down your throat. So the second element of speech is **water**.

With *h* and the vowels, breath and water, we can begin to make words. The first word would be *h* and the first vowel to emerge from the back of the mouth, which is *u: hu*.

Well, that's pretty unremarkable, you might think. *Hu*. Except that *hu* is Sanskrit for 'invoke the gods' and it is the root of our word *God* in English. Now this becomes more interesting. So the first word the human apparatus is capable of pronouncing is Sanskrit for 'invoke the gods' and the root of our word *God*. Does this not imply that we are somehow made to call on God?

If you look in an etymological dictionary, a dictionary that gives you the evolution of words over time, you will find that *human* derives from the Latin *homo*, meaning 'man'. But I would like to suggest that *human* is actually a combination of *hu* and *man*. We are *hu-man*. That is, we are made in God's image and meant to call on him.

Let us continue with our exposition of language. The third element of speech is **flesh**. This is when we obstruct the passage of air with our lips or our tongue and form the consonants. The consonants may or may not have voice added to them, they may be voiced or voiceless. There are seven pairs of consonants, and they are the following: *b-p*, *d-t*, *f-v*, *g-k*, *l-r*, *m-n* and *s-z*. These pairs are incredibly important for an understanding of the spiritual side of language. The letters of each pair are pronounced in a similar part of the mouth. Sometimes, one of them is voiced and the other is voiceless: try pronouncing *b-p* or *d-t*, for example, and you will see what I mean. Only *l-r* and *m-n* are always voiced.

The important thing to remember with the consonants is that we have obstructed the passage of air with our lips or tongue to make these sounds, whether or not voice is added.

So far, we have looked at twenty letters: *h*, five vowels and fourteen consonants. There are also three semi-vowels, where the air is only partially obstructed. Each semi-vowel corresponds to a vowel. The semi-vowels *j* and *y* correspond to the vowel *i*, while the semi-vowel *w* corresponds to the vowel *u*. The last three letters – c, q and *x* – are what I would call redundant letters because they represent sounds that have already been included. The letter c is pronounced *k* or *s*; q is pronounced *k*; and *x* is pronounced *ks*. So we don't really need these letters. It is important to remember here that c can be pronounced *k/s*, that is it can refer to either of these two sounds.

That is the English alphabet: *h*, five vowels, fourteen consonants, three semi-vowels (*i-j/y, u-w*) and three redundant letters (*c-k/s, q-k, x-ks*).

The three elements of speech represented by these letters – breath (*h*), water (vowels) and flesh (consonants) – are also the three elements of creation found in the account of creation in the first two chapters of the Book of Genesis. Let us look at the creation of man in chapter 2:

> A *stream* would rise from the *earth*, and *water* the whole face of the *ground* – then the LORD God formed man from the *dust* of the ground, and *breathed* into his nostrils the *breath* of life, and the man became a living being. (Gen 2:6-7, NRSV, my italics)

Do you see how the three elements of speech are included here? Breath, water/stream, and flesh/earth/ground/dust. It took these three elements to make man. That is, God spoke the world into being. In chapter 1 of Genesis, each paragraph begins, 'And God said...' I think this is literally true. God spoke the sky, the earth, the sun and moon, fish and birds, animals and humans into being. Is there anything in language to confirm this?

Well, yes, there is. If we remember that the letter c can be pronounced *k/s*, we will see that there is a clear correlation between the words *space* and *speak* if we rearrange the letters slightly.

What is it God spoke into being? The world. *World* is a combination of two words: *word* and *lord*. 'And God said.'

When was the earth created? On day three. It is interesting that *earth* in reverse is *three*, if we keep the consonantal cluster *th* together and allow fluidity to the vowels (*a-e*), after all they are water. So the word itself, *earth*, seems to be telling us that it was created on day *three*. It is also planet number three in order of increasing distance from the sun. And three as a number is clearly related to the Christian concept of the Holy Trinity (Father, Son, and Holy Spirit), as it is the number of elements in speech and in creation.

Finally, there is one word that the elements of breath, water and flesh have in common. Apart from the seven pairs of consonants (or phonetic pairs) I talked about earlier, there is a close correlation between the letters *b*, *v* and *w*. We see this in languages like Greek (where *b* is pronounced *v*), Spanish (*v* is pronounced *b*), Latin (*v* is pronounced *w*) and

German (*w* is pronounced *v*). And this enables me, through *v*, to connect *b/w* with the letter *f*.

We will then see that *breath*, if we rearrange the letters, spells *father*. *Water* is also in *father* if we remove the letter for breath, *h*. And so is *flesh* if we use the phonetic pair *l-r*, take a step in the alphabet (*s-t*) and remove the letter *a*. The word *father* is common to all three elements of speech/creation.

Language is like a fruit. When it becomes ripe, it opens up to us and reveals its contents. These connections between *space* and *speak*, *world*, *word* and *lord*, *earth* and *three*, *father*, *breath*, *water* and *flesh*, have nothing to do with etymology, the science of the evolution of words over time, they have nothing to do with our individual will. No human decided to call the earth 'earth' because in reverse it was similar to the word 'three'. This didn't happen and, even if it had, they would have found it difficult to convince the rest of the human race to follow suit.

This is why I think of these word connections as vertical, not horizontal (over time). This spiritual aspect of language cuts through time and reveals something of eternity.

SECOND LESSON

Alpha and Omega

The problem of this world is that we like to think of ourselves as authors. We like to think that things belong to us, they start with us, whereas in fact they pass through us (or we pass through them). We are translators. Air, for example, when we breathe, passes through us. It does not begin with us and we did not create it. When we breathe, we take what we need (oxygen) and expel what we do not need (carbon dioxide). It is a similar process with eating. We can cook what we like, we can make all sorts of combinations, but if the basic ingredients are missing, there is nothing we can do. We cannot create an onion or a carrot out of nothing. So again, we are translators. We take whatever exists and transform it in some way (hopefully for the better), but without the basic ingredients, without the building materials, we cannot do very much, we are left empty-handed. When we eat, as when we breathe, we take what we need from the food for energy and expel what we do not need, so the food literally passes through us.

It is the same with conversations. We take part in a conversation, but it couldn't really be said that the conversation began with us. The conversation began a long time ago, we just came along at one stage and took part in it. When people speak, we endeavour to decipher their meaning. The words go in our ears, we take what we need to decipher the meaning (at least, the meaning as we understand it) and expel the rest (the words that we do not need, the pauses, the ums and ahs).

Even life, that most precious commodity, passes through us. We do not put the seed in our balls, the eggs in our wombs, they are already there. We receive life from our parents and pass it on to our children, we *translate* life from one generation to the next. But we are not the authors of life. It does not begin with us. We cannot breathe life into an inanimate object, as God can. God is the author; we are translators.

We take what already exists (a text in the source language), we work on that text (look up unknown words in the dictionaries, consult with the author or with an expert in their work, make sure we understand the whole as best as we can) and then we transfer that text into another language, so that the readers of another language can understand it. The text passes through us – a magical moment, because in this moment, after the horizontal work of preparation, the text has to disappear in order to reappear in another language, where does it go when this happens? – and acquires new meaning in another language. We also extract meaning from the process, we are not the same as before we translated the text, it influences our outlook, our understanding. So meaning is a two-way process. It works both ways. We give and receive meaning during any transaction.

But we think we are authors. We think things belong to us if we pay for them. Actually they will stay with us for a while and then we will leave them behind when we die, so I couldn't really say they belong to us for very long. When we claim ownership, we tend to draw lines. A wall around a property, for example. Borders around a country. The danger is once you draw a line and claim ownership, you are inviting conflict, because what happens when someone crosses that line with hostile intent? You must either reach an agreement with that person or go to war. Laws have been enacted – I am talking about human laws, because there is a vast difference between divine and human law – to protect the right to property, in effect to avoid the need to go to war. This is why the words *law* and *war* are connected by one of the pairs of consonants I talked about in the previous lesson, *l-r*. Human law exists to avoid the need to go to war, to avoid conflict, though it doesn't always work out like that, when treaties are broken, when people transgress the law and decide to cross the line anyway. This is why *law* in reverse (a very common way to make word connections is to read the word in reverse, as we did with *earth-three*) is *wall*. The law acts as a wall, a virtual wall, but one that can feel very real.

So as soon as we draw a line, we invite conflict, whether we want to or not. It is a result of claiming to be authors. It is also the source of a great deal of stress. As soon as you lay aside the claim to ownership, you can relax your grip, the worries and concerns (insurance, potential dangers, potential threats) fade away because you realize that your position in the world is not what you thought it was. You are in effect just passing through, and your purpose is to give and receive meaning, to be a vehicle for love, to show kindnesses. I think we all reach an understanding of this, but if you were to listen to the news, you would think the raison d'être of human existence was economics.

Economics is the result of teaching our children to count up from the number 1. This is a fatal mistake and has untold consequences. When you start counting up from the number 1, there is literally no end, you can go on for ever. The number 1 is a kind of line. If you rotate it by ninety degrees, it is also a closed eye. This is because it represents spiritual blindness.

We take what the earth provides – there isn't much else we can take – we claim it as our own and proceed to trade in it. The earth provides a commodity, there is a constant flow of this commodity – if there isn't, then production will stop and the factory or whatever it is will go out of business. In grammatical terms, this constant flow can be called *uncountable*. It goes on seemingly for ever. Think of oil gushing out of the ground or grain flowing through a hopper. What we do when we trade is take something that is uncountable, that goes on seemingly for ever, and make it *countable*. We package it so that we can sell it. We put the commodity in a bottle, a can, a plastic bag. We draw a line around it so that we can control the flow and count how much is coming in and how much is going out. The earth doesn't do this. It doesn't limit the flow of things (unless we abuse it). Instead of acting like translators and enabling the flow for the greater good of people, we control the flow. We even sometimes cut off the flow when this will increase our profits. By drawing a line around the product so that we can sell it, we are in effect defining it. Definition is to draw a line around something. We count the number of bottles, cans, bags, and charge for them. This is the result of teaching our children to count up from 1. It is the same mentality.

And it is our definition – the packaging – causing such enormous problems to the environment. It is the way we draw a line around something in order to control the flow, the way we turn something uncountable into something countable so that we can trade in it and make a profit, that leads to rubbish, because what is inside the packaging is generally consumed, but the packaging is not. So I would say the waste causing so many problems to our planet is a direct result of human definition, of counting.

There is something else that closely resembles a line, just as the number 1 does, and that is the ego: I. It is remarkable that the ego in English is represented by a line. I would say that we live now in the era of the ego, of the I. This is a result of the Fall, which is recounted after the creation story, in chapter 3 of the Book of Genesis, when Adam and Eve were expelled from Paradise. The I, if we rotate it by ninety degrees, is a closed eye. See how close the words *Eve* and *eye* are, all we have done is continue the letter *v*. The two words, *eye* and *I*, sound the same, and I think this is for a reason, because the I represents a closed eye.

We live in the era of the I, with each person having to defend their own interests (instead of looking after the interests of others, which is what we should be doing). Now that we are here, with our separate properties, our separate bank accounts, our separate belongings, what do we do? How do we escape the line that is represented by the number 1 or the pronoun I? How do we open our spiritual eyes?

There are three ways to escape the line: 1 or I. The first is to make reference to a third point, so that the conversation is no longer just between you and me, but involves a third person. We make reference to the source, as if when crossing a river we bear in mind the source of that river up in the mountains. When we do this, we make something much more stable than a wall or a tower. We make a pyramid. We make a triangle. What letter is it in the alphabet that represents a triangle? It is the letter A (a triangle on stilts).

The second way to escape the line is simply to draw a line through it. This makes a cross: †. The Christian symbol of the cross is a deleted ego, whereby we turn from the ego to God (this is why *God* and *ego* are only a step in the alphabet, *d-e*, apart). But Christianity is a religion of paradox. Christ tells us we must lose our life in order to find it: 'Those who find their life will lose it, and those who lose their life for my sake will find it' (Mt 10:39). How can this be? How can you lose your life – sacrifice yourself for the other – and yet find it? This doesn't make sense. Well, when we draw a line through the ego and make a cross, we also make a plus-sign: +. This is the meaning of losing your life in order to find it, and Christ expands on this in Mark 10:29-31. So the second way to escape the line is to make a cross/plus-sign.

And the third way is to do precisely what we do not teach our children in school: to count down. So many problems in this world would be avoided if we only taught our children not to count up (to make a profit), but to count down. It is also much shorter! When we count down from 1, we reach 0, an eternal symbol that goes on for ever, a symbol that represents God. This is why the word G O D, if we write it in capital letters, resembles three Os, the Holy Trinity.

So the three ways of escaping the line – and I don't think there's any other way of doing this – give rise to three symbols – A + O – a triangle, a cross or a plus-sign and the number 0. When we count down from the number 1 and open our (spiritual) eyes, we open the line, we put space in it.

When we turn away from the demands of the ego, we allow space in our lives to God. We believe in him (there is no other way to have faith). And we call upon his name, because the symbols A + O spell the name of God found in the Book of Revelation, the last book in the Bible, that is Alpha and Omega. These three symbols are found in the middle conjunction of the name 'Alpha and Omega', that is 'and', which, if we write it with capital letters, can be read A 'N' D. The reverse of *and* is *DNA*: it is in our DNA to do this.

Just as we saw in the first lesson that a *hu-man* is made to call on God (remember that *hu* is the root of our word *God*), so *I* am made to call on God. If you want to escape the demands of the ego, there is actually no other place to go, as language would tell us.

AIO

When we cut off the flow of something, when we take something that the earth produces and package it, when we draw a line around it – that is, when we define it – we do this in order to engage in trade, to buy and sell, to make a profit. We turn something constant, something that flows without end – that is, something uncountable – into something countable. Let us take an example. Oil flows constantly, we cannot sell oil as it is, so we package it in a bottle or a barrel, and we sell those bottles or barrels. Rice flows constantly, but in order to sell it, we must weigh it in some way – a kilo – or package it in some way – a bag. Water flows constantly. Again, in order to sell it, we must put it in a bottle, or else it will slip through our fingers. When we make something uncountable countable in this way, when we draw a line around something in order to package it, there is a word that appears in English: *a* or *an*, the indefinite article. Things that are uncountable – air, water, love, righteousness (often they are concepts, things that we cannot quite grasp) – are not preceded by the indefinite article. Only when we package them, when we draw a line around them, when we *define* them, can they be preceded by the indefinite article: a bottle, a bag, a barrel, a can. Think of metal. We mine metal from the earth; it only becomes countable when we talk about a specific vein, or when we talk about a product made with the metal, such as a car.

This word, *a* or *an*, is extremely important, because it indicates that we have separated something off in some way. Love is a concept. It is also a reality. You cannot separate love off. Things that are uncountable do not begin with us, we are not their authors, they flow through us, as I explained in the second lesson. It is only when we stop the flow, when we claim something for ourselves, that things become countable and we can count them, just as we teach our children to count up from 1.

So I would say we make things countable in order to exert some kind of control over them, in order to quantify them, in order to control their flow. There is an extremely important verse in the Bible, for me it is probably the most important verse in the Old Testament, Exodus 3:14. God sends Moses to free the Israelites from Egyptian rule. Moses asks who he is to say has sent him, he can't just turn up and tell the Israelites to leave, the Egyptians to let them go, he has to do this on someone's authority. God replies by telling him who has sent him:

> God said to Moses, 'I AM WHO I AM.' He said further, 'Thus you shall say to the Israelites, "I AM has sent me to you."' (Ex 3:14, NRSV)

Here we see God's name for the first time: AM or I AM. This name is extremely important. Anyone who has studied Greek will know that there are two os in Greek, a short o (omicron) and a long o (omega), which is the last letter in the Greek alphabet. This is why in the Book of Revelation God calls himself Alpha and Omega, because he is the beginning and the end (the first and last letters of the alphabet). Omega in Greek is written with a *w*. We might see that this name of God, Alpha and Omega, which we talked about in the previous lesson, is also present in *AM* if we simply turn the *M* upside down: *AW*. There are other connections. For example, *AM* in reverse is *ma*, which is Sanskrit for 'create'.

You may remember that I talked about seven pairs of consonants, which are extremely important for an understanding of the spiritual side of language. One of these pairs is *m-n*. If we apply this pair to *AM*, we get *an*, the indefinite article. When God created man, he separated him off in some way (of course, you can never be quite separate from God, because God has no borders, he is not limited in any way). He made man countable. But he didn't do this in order to trade in man. He did this for a much more exalted reason: to give him free will. Now man could decide on his actions, could choose to acquiesce or to deny, to go this way or that, to remain in Paradise or to be expelled. But this was necessary in order that man could choose to love God freely, to believe in him, to make space for him by expanding the line.

So *AM* created *an*. If we put these two words together, we get *a man*. The name of that man was *ADAM*. Again, we see the presence of Alpha and Omega in the man's name: *AO*, *AW*. We carry God's imprint, we are made in his image and likeness (Gen 1:26). I believe that the act of creation recounted in the first two chapters of Genesis is closely linked to the letter A, the first letter of the alphabet ('In the beginning...', Gen 1:1).

Having created man, God then brought the creatures to him to see what he would call them. He didn't ask man to create the creatures, that was God's job, he is the author. He asked him to name them, and see how *name* is *man* in reverse with the addition of *e*. It also spells *mean* and *amen* if we rearrange the letters. He asked man to give the creatures meaning and, by acquiescing in this act, man agreed, he said 'amen' to God's will, in effect he became a translator by deciding what word to use.

In the Fall, however, recounted in chapter 3 of Genesis, man went against God's will and ate of the fruit of the tree of the knowledge of good and evil, something God had told him not to do. He made the progression from A to I. Instead of calling on God's name, *AM*, he said *I'm*. Instead of saying *amen* to God's will, he said *mine*.

Instead of deciding *what* to call the creatures, he asked the fateful question *why*. Why should I do this? Why should I believe you? We think of the question word *why* as asserting our freedom, our right to choose. It actually reveals a lack of faith. If you question something, you are asserting your own will. This is why obedience (there are many examples of this among the desert fathers of the fourth century) is so important in monasticism, because it shows humility and trust.

So man made the progression from A to I, he turned away from God, and we see this progression in the name of his helpmate, *Eve*, which is closely linked to *eye* (*v*-*y*, a pair of letters that look alike), a word that sounds the same as *I*.

This is where we are at the moment, in the era of the I. We looked in the previous lesson at the three ways of escaping the I by making reference to a third point (A), by deleting the I (+), by treating it as a number and counting down (O). In terms of the alphabet, we are now called to make the progression from I to O. So instead of saying *I'm*, we say *om*, a mantra used in Hinduism and Tibetan Buddhism, but that is not what I mean. For me, *om* is a reference to the Holy Trinity, three in One: O_3 (see the next lesson). If we apply the same phonetic pair we used earlier, *m-n*, and add an *e*, we can turn *om* into *no one*, a reference to God the Father (again, see the next lesson). Instead of saying *mine*, we say *omen* or *nemo*. *Nemo* is the Latin word for 'no one', which gives the same result as *I'm-om-no one*. Instead of saying *why*, we realize that the all-important question in this life is *who*.

Let us pause a little. When Pontius Pilate is dealing with Christ before the latter's crucifixion, they start to have a slightly philosophical conversation, and Pilate asks,

'What is truth?' (Jn 18:38). Pilate has not made the progression from A to I to O. If he had made the progression, he would have realized that the real question is *who* and he would have asked, 'Who is truth?' And then, quite possibly, Christ would have answered, 'I am'. As it is, Christ remained silent, because Pilate hadn't realized that truth is not a thing, it is a person, and he was standing in front of him.

We might also observe that *who* sounds exactly the same as the Sanskrit word we saw in the first lesson that means 'invoke the gods' and is the root of our word *God*, that is *hu*.

It is also found in some icons of Christ as the Greek translation of the name God says to Moses in the verse from Exodus I quoted earlier: 'I AM WHO I AM.' In Greek, this name is translated as 'ἐγώ εἰμι ὁ ὤν' (literally, 'I am the being'). The last three letters of this translation are included in icons of Christ as O WN, because it is understood that all appearances of God in the Old Testament are by the Logos, that is by Christ himself. In Slavonic countries (where I live), the letter N is written H, the two letters are very similar, and a stylized N can look very like an H. We might also notice that there is a rough breathing on the first of the two words in Greek, 'ὁ ὤν', that little c sitting on top of the letter o, which is how Greek represents the letter h. So I have seen O WN, the name of God in Exodus, written O WH, which with the letters rearranged spells the question words who and how, the answer to which is a person.

So who is an incredibly important word: it sounds the same as hu and it contains the Greek translation of the name of God in Exodus 3:14, 'I AM'. It fulfils both these ancient names of God. But there is a third name that it also fulfils: the Hebrew Tetragrammaton, YHWH (sometimes written Yahweh). This name of God, found in the Old Testament, YHWH, is incredibly close to the question word we talked about earlier, why. It contains the same letters. The progression from I to O (remember that the semi-vowel y corresponds to i) gives us who, or O WH, the Greek translation of 'I AM' found in icons of Christ, whose life and teachings are the subject of the New Testament. It is as if Christ fulfils the Old Testament and shows us the way to go.

We find this same progression from I to O, away from the ego, in other words, too. Think of the word *live*. If we turn this word around, if we distort its purpose, so to speak, we get *evil*. This is one choice open to us in this life: to do evil. But if we count down from I to O, if we remove the ego represented in English by the letter *I*, we get *love*. We take the ego out of the equation, we take ourselves out of the equation, we cease to be authors and make ourselves translators, vehicles of love.

The same thing happens with *sin*. Instead of opting to *sin*, we take away the ego, count down from I to O and choose to become a *son*, a co-heir of the kingdom. Even *Christ*, who was without sin himself, made this progression by going to the *cross*.

This is the progression that we are called to make: from the A of creation to the I of the Fall to the O of repentance. 'O' is an exclamation. It is a realization. We breathe space into the line, as if we were opening a bag, and our spiritual eyes (our spiritual Is) are opened.

The Latin alphabet does not make this progression. The Latin alphabet goes from A to

I to Z. It counts up, because the letter Z closely resembles the number 2. I understand this to refer to a Western way of thinking, based on rationalism, reliance on the self. The Greek alphabet, however, which represents a more philosophical, theological way of thinking, does make this progression. The last letter of the Greek alphabet is omega, the letter O.

If we write omega using the Greek letter W, we find this same progression from A to I to O (W) in the name of God in Exodus, *I AM* (you have to turn the *M* upside down). We also find it in *law* (lower-case *l* closely resembles upper-case *I*). I understand this to be the law of the Old Testament. And we find it in *way* (remember *y* corresponds to *i*). This is a reference to Christ in the New Testament, when he says, '*I am* the *way*, and the truth, and the life' (Jn 14:6, my italics). He means this literally. He is the answer to the question words we should be asking: *who* and *how*. That is why he continues, 'No one comes to the Father except through me.'

One

So we breathe life into the line, I, and make it an O. Perhaps this is the only way we can imitate God in the act of creation, by breathing life into our own ego. I have often thought this act of counting down from 1 to 0, of taking the ego out of the equation, is represented by an exclamation mark, ! There is the line and, below it, the circle. It is also represented by a question mark, ?, only by asking questions it takes longer to reach the destination. It is like a keyhole, a line, but where we insert the key is a circle. We turn the key and the door opens.

We cannot go back to A, as we cannot re-enter our mother's womb. I believe that we are meant to go onwards. Now that we have entered the Fall, I, we must make the progression to O. It is interesting for me that three Os together are found in the word G O D. I wonder what three Is together would spell?

Fathers of the Church have struggled to explain the Christian concept of the Holy Trinity. How can God be three in one? Surely, that is paradoxical. Well, I think a lot of Christianity is paradoxical – we must lose our life in order to find it; the last will be first, and the first will be last. You wonder how this can be. But I begin to think that paradox is a sign of the truth.

It will be easier to understand this concept of 'three in one' if we write the number one using capital letters: ONE. It is interesting for me that the number one begins precisely with a circle. And if we write it using capital letters, ONE, we can see that the word contains three numbers, but the number it doesn't contain is itself: 1. It contains 0, 2 (on its side) and 3 (back to front).

So I believe that the Trinity is literally three in ONE. Imagine we are dealing with chemical formulas. God the Father would be O_1, except that in chemistry the subscript $_1$ is not normally written down. So God the Father would be O. If we include the subscript, O_1, we could say that God the Father is 'no one', the result of the progression from A to I to O we saw in the previous lesson: *AM-I'm-om, no one; amen-mine-nemo* (Latin for 'no one').

The Greek word for 'God', *theos*, seems to confirm this. If we omit the final *s* (as happens in modern Greek and in the vocative), we get *theo*. So we could say that God in Greek is 'the O'.

God the Son, that is Jesus Christ, would be O_2. We could liken him to oxygen. I wonder if he can be likened to other aspects of nature. Well, it is surely an enormous coincidence that the words 'Son' and 'sun' sound exactly the same. And if we think of the nine planets (I still include Pluto) as being numbered from 1 to 9 (with earth being planet number three, as we saw in the first lesson), then the sun would be 0. The way we count is in the stars, but note that the stars count from 0 to 9 (not 1 to 10).

And the Holy Spirit, the Comforter, would be O_3, the chemical formula for ozone, that layer that protects the earth from the sun's rays.

Three in ONE: $O_{(1)}$, O_2, O_3. The number that *ONE* doesn't contain is the ego, I. It is also extremely similar to the Greek translation of 'I AM' found in icons of Christ: *O WN* (we only have to rotate the E).

The Holy Spirit in Greek is called 'breath', *pneuma*. It is likened to the wind, which is how the Holy Spirit descends at Pentecost (Acts 2:1-4). So we could also represent it by the letter *h*. If we put the Holy Spirit, H, and God the Son, O_2, together, we get H_2O, the chemical formula for water. So I would suggest that we receive our light and warmth from God (the sun/Son), we breathe God (oxygen/O_2) and we drink God (water/H_2O). It is curious that the moon, if we write it with capital letters, MOON, is also a combination of Christ and the Holy Spirit – O_2 and O_3 (the 2 is on its side, the 3 is on its front) – and the moon is said to be 230,000 miles from the earth, whose axis is 23°. This combination of Christ and the Holy Spirit can be found widely in nature.

And as we found three Os in G O D, so we can find three Os in the word WOOD, except that WOOD has the number 3 (on its back) at the beginning. I hardly need specify the relevance of WOOD to Christianity in terms of the tree in Eden and the cross, its ultimate symbol.

So I would hazard that language is Trinitarian. The words themselves seem to confirm this. I don't think I'm making anything up, I'm simply analyzing their content.

I believe that Christ is the Son of God, the Only-Begotten. He came down to earth in order to translate for us the meaning of life (he did this by means of parables, stories that seem to be about somebody else, but are in fact about us). How does an author – God – become a translator? By becoming human. So he became human, he was incarnate of the Holy Spirit and the Virgin Mary, not only so that we could go in the opposite direction and become gods by grace (a process known as *theosis*), but also so that he could translate for us. We hadn't understood the purpose of life (to count down from I to O), we lived in darkness, we had only glimpsed certain aspects of faith, but God himself was unknown to us until he came in the flesh.

Now I am going to go back to those seven pairs of consonants, because there are two very beautiful words found in *Christ*, but we have to apply the phonetic pairs. The first is *child* (phonetic pairs *d-t* and *l-r*, addition of *s*). If you take away the letter *s*, it can be seen that *Christ* contains *child*, and indeed he became a child in order to come into the world. We must also become children in terms of trust if we want to enter the kingdom of heaven, as Christ himself tells us (Mt 18:3).

The second is *light* (phonetic pairs *g-k* and *l-r*, addition of *s*; remember that c corresponds to *k*). There is a painting by William Holman Hunt – Christ *The Light of the World*. In the long succession of passages in John's Gospel where Christ tells us who he is ('I am...'), in one of them, Christ says, 'I am the light of the world' (Jn 8:12). Again, I think he means this literally. He is somehow the light of the world. Without him, we are in darkness. Is there any other evidence in language for the correlation between Christ and light, between Son and sun? Well, another appellation Christ receives, from John the Baptist in John 1:29, is the Lamb of God. He is seen as a sacrificial lamb who sacrifices himself for our sakes, who gives himself as a ransom

satisfies us and takes away that empty feeling that is produced by the things of this world, which always need refilling. He is the bread of life, 'a spring of water gushing up to eternal life' (Jn 4:14).

As when we place three Os together, we get G O D, so when we place three Is together, we get *I l l*. We become *ill* when we are apart from God, when we turn our backs on him.

Love

In counting down from I to O, in turning *live* into *love* and *sin* into *son*, we lay aside the demands of the ego, a self-centred approach to life, and we acknowledge the existence and importance of the other. This is the process every human must go through. I would say that the world is a training ground. It exists not in its perfect state for us to learn the importance of the other and to grow spiritually. As we spend nine months in our mother's womb in order to have a physical birth, so we must spend three score years and ten in this world to have a spiritual birth, to be spoken into eternity. The world is a spiritual womb, just as our mother's womb is a physical womb. But the spiritual part takes longer, just as spiritual blindness lasts longer than physical blindness. The problem with spiritual blindness is that, just like the person who makes noise, we don't realize we're spiritually blind and we think we can see perfectly.

Language points us away from the demands of the ego, it points us to a collective standpoint, the body of the Church. We become part of something bigger and, instead of making up our own sentences, we begin to repeat the sentences of others, prayers that were written seventeen hundred years ago. We find solace in repetition. Every Sunday, we go to church and repeat the same words and, as we repeat them, we go deeper, just as rubbing away at a surface enables us to go deeper, we sink into the words, and they effect a change in us. So we go from originality, the desire to be original, to non-originality. Actually, in many ways, we don't want to be original anymore, we accept that we are translators and things pass through us (air, food, words), just as we pass through them (the house, the world we live in, experiences that come our way).

The self decreases in stature in order to be reborn spiritually. We become who we truly are, no longer a slave to the passions of anger, lust, pride and greed. We achieve this through the other. We cannot do it on our own, in isolation. We are saved through the other, who prays for us, has a stake in our lives and returns us to ourself.

Let us look at the word *self*. In reverse, it spells *flesh* with the addition of *h*. The *self* must go the way of all *flesh*. It is *false* (addition of *a*). When we listen to its demands, it actually takes us somewhere we do not want to go. It turns us into a *slave* (phonetic pair *f-v*). We realize that what we took to be our decisions were actually things over which we had no control. We have become addicted to a certain way of living, to a particular vice, and now that we want to, we cannot get away from it, because we have become enslaved to it.

When we have this feeling that we're not giving in willingly, but have actually become subjected to something against our own will, when we begin to resist, to put up a fight, upon realizing that the freedom to do whatever we like, whatever the cost, is not actually freedom at all, then we have begun to repent, to turn our minds in another direction, to seek a way out. We turn from the *ego* to *God*, we place someone else at the centre of our lives. This is a major moment, and also a source of immense relief. We no longer have to carry the burden, because it is no longer all about us. There is a short sentence in the Gospel, spoken by Christ: 'You cannot serve God and wealth' (Mt 6:24). The Greek word for 'wealth' is *mammon*. It is extraordinary for me that if we take the word *money* and read it in reverse, we get *venom* (*v-y*). Money can be a source of great conflict. Another word for 'money' might be 'gold'. Do you see how close *God* and *gold* are? I think this relates to the sentence I have just quoted from Matthew's Gospel. What separates them? A single letter: the ego, I.

So too, if we remove the ego from *slave*, we get *save*. In both cases, salvation is possible. We apply two of the phonetic pairs I talked about in the first lesson, *f-v* and *l-r*, to the word *self* and find *serve* (repetition of *e*). The way to escape the demands of the *self* is to *serve*. Who do we serve? The other. And how do we do this? With love.

There is a famous passage on love in St Paul's First Letter to the Corinthians, chapter 13, which is often read at weddings. But the word itself will give us a pretty good definition of what it is. *Love* is *low*. It is humble. It does not place itself first. *Love* is *oval*. I find oval to be a very humble gesture, as when we clasp our hands in prayer. *Love* takes us away from *I owe* to a realization of the other: *I, o we!* We realize that we are greater as part of the collective than on our own. Love does not speak the language of debt. In fact, *debt* as a word is clearly related to *death* (a step in the alphabet, *a-b*, addition of *h*). *Love* enables us to *evolve*.

Love makes us *whole* (*v-w*, addition of *h*). This is a very important connection. Without the presence of the letters *v-w*, all we have is a *hole*. We feel an emptiness in our lives, something that cannot be filled, however much food or liquid we pour into it. What we need is the Trinity, the presence of the number 3 at the beginning of the word, to make us whole. *Whole* is also a combination of another name of God in the Old Testament, *El*, and the Greek translation of 'I AM' found in icons of Christ: *O WH*. Again, we see Christ as the one who makes us whole. I am not being evangelical, I am simply stating a fact.

But there are even more beautiful connections than these. Language is a dance. It offers us unfamiliar perspectives, it takes us where we do not dare to go. *Love, evolve, low, oval.* If we take a step in the alphabet (*t-v*, omitting the vowel *u*), apply the phonetic pair *l-r* and add the letter *h*, *love* gives *other*. We cannot love on our own, just as we cannot have children on our own. There is a reason for this. And *other*, if we take another step in the alphabet (*r-s*), gives us the Greek word for 'God', *theos*:

love – other – theos

'On these two commandments hang all the law and the prophets.' Thus says Christ in Matthew 22:40. A lawyer has just asked him which is the greatest commandment of them all, and Christ has replied, 'You shall love the Lord your God with all your heart, and with all your soul, and with all your mind' (*love-theos*). He then gives a second commandment, 'You shall love your neighbour as yourself' (*love-other*).

And only a few chapters later, in the Judgement of the Nations, he explains that the other is in fact God: 'Just as you did it to one of the least of these who are members of my family, you did it to me' (Mt 25:40). That is to say any kindness we show to another, from sharing our food to giving them a glass of water, it is as if we had done it to God himself (*other-theos*).

So for me the whole content of the Christian Gospel is contained in these connections: *love – other – theos*. Love the Lord your God with all your heart; love your neighbour as yourself.

And there is one other word that is connected to love. It is a word that we have been using a lot. We must apply the phonetic pair *l-r* and also *v-w*, and take a step in the alphabet, *d-e*. *Love* is connected to *word*. We would do well to remember this every time we open our mouth to speak! Can you imagine what a world it would be if every word was spoken with love? Well, language doesn't seem to have a problem with this. In fact, it seems to be pointing us in precisely that direction.

So *love* is connected with *whole*, with *other* and *theos*, and with *word*. And there is a beautiful connection in the first three letters of *word*. If we take a step in the alphabet, *r-s*, we find *sow* in reverse. This is a clear reference to the Parable of the Sower, found earlier in Matthew, chapter 13, where the sower goes out to sow. Some seed lands on the path, where it cannot take root. The seed is the word of the kingdom. This means the person who hears it doesn't understand. Some seed falls on rocky ground. This means the person who hears it receives it with joy, but later loses interest. Some seed lands among thorns. This means the person is too weighed down by the cares of this world and the lure of wealth to make room for it. And some seed falls on good soil, where it takes root and grows. This is the person who is receptive to the word of the kingdom and makes room for it in their life. We have to be able to hear in order to understand. It is not enough just to open our ears and let the words pass through and out the other end, we have to act on them.

The parable that follows this is the Parable of the Tares, which is again about the sowing of seed. A householder sows seed in his field to grow wheat, but an enemy comes in the night and sows weeds among the wheat. His slaves ask him if he wants them to uproot the weeds, but he says no, because they may uproot the wheat as well. They will wait until harvest time and reap them both. The wheat they will gather into the barn, whereas the weeds they will set on fire. This is a reference to the kingdom of heaven. We grow alongside one another, but at the end of time God will send his angels to bring in the harvest. Those who have done good – the wheat – will be gathered into his barn (the kingdom of heaven), whereas the evildoers – the weeds – will be thrown into the furnace of fire. Christ ends the parable by exclaiming, 'Let anyone with ears listen!' (Mt 13:43).

It is curious that we have ears, and so does wheat. We have to be able to hear. That is, we have to be receptive. The only way to do this is to believe. If you do not believe in God, if you do not believe that we live in a greater context than mere economics and fulfilling our physical needs, then you cannot be receptive to his word. This often involves some kind of spiritual experience, or it can be through meeting another person who is themselves a believer.

Ear is in *hear*, just as *eyes* contains *see*. This is a coincidence, but what is an even greater coincidence is that *hear* is in *heart*, just as *see* is in *seed*.

So where does the seed have to be planted? In our heart (not in our head, God does not require us to rationalize, he wants us to believe!).

This is why the letters of *heart* rearranged spell *earth*. The seed is to be planted in the *earth* of our *heart*. Or in the *soil* of our *soul*.

I think language understands this better than we do. If we are prepared to look beyond mere appearances, to look beneath the surface, to enter the words as if they were buildings and admire their construction, their columns and flutes, their aisles and apses, to turn them around, to see how they change in the angled light, we will gain a new perspective. But what is certain is that we did not put this information in the words, just as we did not create the planet on which we live. They were already there, before we were born. This is why I think language and the environment have a lot in common. They both contain a hidden meaning, which is slowly revealed when we have ears to listen.

Believe

We have seen that Christianity is a religion of paradox, and paradox might be taken as an indicator of truth. Christ died and rose again. That is a kind of paradox. He went through death, death was not an end in itself, he descended into Hades (*Hades*, the place a *shade* inhabits, a word closely connected with *death* and *earth*) and later appeared to his disciples before ascending into heaven. He ascended into heaven in order that we might receive the Holy Spirit, in order that the Holy Spirit might fill our lives, something that occurred ten days later, at Pentecost, when the Holy Spirit descended on the apostles and enabled them to speak in many languages. This is not an act altogether removed from translation, by the way.

Christ often speaks in a way that seems paradoxical. I have already cited the example of losing our life in order to find it. We lose our life – that is, we sacrifice our own will and turn away from the demands of the ego in order to serve God's will and our neighbour's needs, we delete the ego (†) – in order to find it (+), because as Christ says, 'there is no one who has left house or brothers or sisters or mother or father or children or fields, for my sake and for the sake of the good news, who will not receive a hundredfold now in this age – houses, brothers and sisters, mothers and children, and fields, with persecutions – and in the age to come eternal life' (Mk 10:29-30). I think we can conclude that a hundredfold followed by eternal life is a plus. The same symbol, the ego with a line drawn through it, can have both negative and positive connotations.

We have also seen how the Holy Trinity can literally be said to be three in ONE, something that also sounds paradoxical. It is paradoxical in the same way that a mother and father coming together to give birth to a child, which can be represented in mathematical terms as $1 + 1 = 1$, is also paradoxical (three in ONE). There are some beautiful connections here, because *birth* is connected with *child* (a step in the alphabet, *b-c*, phonetic pairs *d-t* and *l-r*) and also with *third* (pair of letters that look alike, *b-d*).

Straight after elucidating what those who follow him will receive, Christ says, 'But many who are first will be last, and the last will be first' (Mk 10:31). Now this is surely paradoxical, and I wonder how it can be explained. The first will be last, and the last will be first. This sentence also comes at the end of the Parable of the Workers in the Vineyard (Mt 20:1-16), in which those who have been working in the vineyard since morning and have endured the scorching heat receive the same daily wage that those who turned up at five o'clock received. They are a little miffed, understandably, but they have received what they were owed. It's just that other people who didn't do the same amount of work have received the same. The landowner, who I think we can take to be a representation of God, explains that that's his business, whether he decides to give the same reward to one as to the other. And I suppose we can understand working in the vineyard to refer to the amount of time we have been active in the faith, receiving a hundredfold, but with that slightly worrying addendum, 'with persecutions', which I take to refer to the endurance of troubles that are an accompaniment to faith and repentance.

Here is how I understand this apparent paradox. The desire to be first leads to conflict (we cannot all be first). *First*, as a word, is clearly linked to *fist* and to *strife*, so the outcome of wishing to be first is pretty clear to see, though that doesn't stop us extolling the virtues of competition (a strange concept, and one that I never understood fully – shouldn't we be helping the other, rather than trying to push them down into the mud?).

What is *first* has a *thirst* – a thirst to come out on top, but also what is newborn, like a baby, always has a thirst, initially a thirst for its mother's milk, later that thirst may manifest itself in other ways. We have made a quarter of a revolution.

What makes us thirst, in particular, is salt (half a revolution). If you eat salt, you will have a raging thirst. So there is a connection between thirst and salt. But *salt* also makes us *last* (three quarters of a revolution). We use salt, for example, in the preservation of meat. So now we have made a connection between first and last, but what is to stop us continually going round in circles, like poor Sisyphus, up and down the hill?

We break the cycle. And we do this by removing the letter *a*, so that *last* gives *lst* (a full revolution). The same result, but the connection with thirst is broken. That is, we no longer indulge the passions, we cultivate the virtues and become *lst*, the opposite of *last*, fit for the kingdom. So, 'the first will be last [those who put themselves at the front are not fit for the kingdom], and the last [those who put others before themselves] will be lst.'

The paradox is explained by word connections – it is explained by language itself.

But since Christ is the Word, this shouldn't surprise us. He knows what he is saying.

I would like to give another example of Christ knowing what he is saying. I think Christ has a great sense of humour, but this is largely missed. I imagine you would have to have a great sense of humour when you are the one by whom all things were made, and yet when you come into the world, you are rejected left, right and centre. It is either that, or cry.

And so, in John 7, as the Jewish festival of Booths is approaching, Jesus is in Galilee. His brothers suggest he might like to show some of the wonders he has been doing a little further afield, after all, that's what he's here for, isn't it? And the festival of Booths in Jerusalem would be a wonderful opportunity to do so. Jesus replies, 'No, I don't think so,' but then (something I do very often) he changes his mind and actually goes and does exactly what he has said he is not going to. He hangs around at the festival, getting waylaid by the Jews, who seem to object to anything good being done on the Sabbath, there's a constant threat to his life, or at least that's what the crowd thinks, and when he says he will be with them only a little longer, because he is going to be crucified (!!!), the crowd wonders whether that means he is going to go on a trip to visit the Greeks in the diaspora.

You can imagine the frustration. The message doesn't seem to be getting through. It comes to the last day of the festival. Jesus is standing there (I can just picture this) and, in his frustration, he cries out, 'Let anyone who is thirsty come to me, and let the one who believes in me drink. As the scripture has said, "Out of the believer's heart shall flow rivers of living water"' (Jn 7:37-8). There is a clear link here to the wonderful story of the meeting of Christ and the Samaritan woman in John 4, another example of deadpan humour. At this point, Jesus is on his way to Galilee (a prophet is not without honour except in his own country) and, to go from Judea to Galilee, he has to pass through Samaria. He stops in Sychar at Jacob's well (in modern-day Nablus) and asks a Samaritan woman to give him some water to drink. The Samaritan woman is surprised, Jews don't normally associate with her kind. Jesus explains (and again, one can imagine the sigh that precedes this), 'If you knew who it is you are talking to [read: the one by whom the world was created!], you would ask him and he would give you *living water.*' I am quoting freely here. Note the connection with the other passage in the words 'living water'.

The Samaritan woman then comes out with what must be one of the most incredible observations ever made: how are you going to do that, if you don't even have a bucket? I can see Jesus smiling inwardly. She has a bucket, but Jesus doesn't. Jesus explains that the water he gives, which we might associate with the water of baptism – the combination of Christ (O_2) and the Holy Spirit (H) – becomes in those who receive it 'a spring of water gushing up to eternal life'.

This is literally true. When we activate our baptism through belief and right practice, then I think the water becomes in us a spring gushing up to eternal life, which is our stopping place. And note how close the words *believe* and *receive* are (a step in the alphabet, *b-c*, phonetic pair *l-r*).

All Jesus asks of us is that we believe. This is all he asks. He doesn't want us to stand on our heads. He doesn't want us to turn somersaults in the air. He doesn't want us to run a marathon, though we can do that if we like. He just asks that we believe, and he will do the rest.

Believe is a very rich word. It contains *be* and *live*. If we remember the correlation between *b-v-w*, it also contains *Bible*, where believers go in order to drink. In reverse, *believe* spells *veiled*. These are mysteries, sacraments, they are not obvious to all and sundry, but only to those who approach them with fear and humility.

And there is one further connection in that earth-shattering cry from scripture, 'Out of the believer's heart shall flow rivers of living water.' The word in Greek is not 'heart', it is 'belly', which presumably is taken to mean the seat of the emotions (though I don't quite see why it is not translated as 'belly'). And if we rewind to chapter 3 of the Book of Genesis, we will see that Adam names his wife Eve 'because she was the mother of all who live' (Gen 3:20). There is a footnote in the NRSV edition of the

Bible that I use: 'In Heb *Eve* resembles the word for *living*.'

So there we have it: *believe* is a combination of *belly* and *Eve*. When Christ says, 'Out of the believer's heart [belly] shall flow rivers of living water,' this is literally true, because that is what the word means on a spiritual level. If we limit ourselves to the meaning we give words, and to how they have evolved over time (the science of etymology), we are affording ourselves only a very limited view, just as if we treat the world as a source of pleasure and profit, there for the taking (which seems to be the basis of a lot of human activity), we are again limiting our viewpoint. The world was there before us. It was put there for our good. We pass through it for a limited period of time. Without basic tools and ingredients, there is nothing we can do. But just as God brings Adam the creatures to name in Genesis 2:19, so he puts the world's resources at our disposal to see what we will do with them, what meaning we will give them. We are translators. We take something written in one language and transform it into another. How we do this depends on us, whether we do it with care and love, or with disregard (I have yet to meet a translator who works with disregard). And the act of translation, the one we look down on so much, the one we consider second-rate and hardly worth paying for, may just be crucial when it comes to inheriting eternal life.

Translation

I remember when I was a teacher in Wandsworth, London. Teachers of English use a timeline to teach their students the different tenses. They draw a horizontal line on the whiteboard and mark the tenses: present, past and future. The tenses have different aspects, simple and continuous, depending on whether the action is permanent or temporary. *I live in London* sounds permanent. *I am living in London* doesn't. I have a particular fondness for the perfect – *I have lived in London for ten years* – which bridges the gap between two of the points marked on the line, in this case the present and the past. This sentence means I moved to London ten years ago, I live in London now. So the perfect covers the period between the past and the present.

In English, there are auxiliary verbs. These verbs are used to 'help'. In the present and the past, the auxiliary verb is *do*. For example, to make a question: *Do you like London?* Or to say something in the negative: *I don't like London very much.* It is the same in the past: *Did you do anything special at the weekend? No, I didn't. I decided to stay at home.* So the auxiliary for the present and the past is *do/did*.

The auxiliary for the perfect is *have*. We have already seen an example: *I have lived in London for ten years.* This means I came to London ten years ago and I am still here, so rather than speaking about a point on the timeline (present, past or future), it bridges the gap between two of those points: past and present.

And the auxiliary for the future is *will*. *What will you do this weekend? I will go and see my mother.*

There is a fourth auxiliary, which is used in all the tenses to make the continuous aspect, which is when we want to place emphasis on the moment, on the fact the action is happening right now, or is repeated, or ongoing. This auxiliary is *be*. *I am talking on the phone,* said in a slightly cross voice, indicates that I am talking on the phone right now and would you please be quiet? *I have been taking German lessons recently* indicates that it is a temporary action – I have only just started – and I've done it on several occasions.

It is remarkable for me that the auxiliaries we use to talk about the present, past and future in more objective terms, without placing an emphasis on the moment, on the continuity of the action, are *do, have* and *will*. Is this not somehow reflective of our approach to this life? *Do* implies activity. *Have* implies possession. And *will* implies getting what we want. I would say these three auxiliary verbs are very reflective of much of human activity in this world.

Only the fourth auxiliary, the one that draws out the moment, the one that says what I am doing right now, the one that enlarges the moment and focuses not on regrets about the past or fears for the future, but simply where and with whom we are right now, is *be*. It reminds me of the way we (mistakenly) teach our children to count up from 1, instead of from 0, which would take ourselves out of the equation and lead to greater reflection. Perhaps it isn't necessary always to be active in order to justify our existence. After all, most of us don't take part in the tasks of growing food and building houses, two basic needs. And yet we seem to fill our time with other activities in order to feel we have done something. We seek to justify ourselves. It is very difficult, excruciatingly difficult, to sit still for five minutes. To pray for five minutes without becoming distracted. And yet it is only when we are *silent* that we can *listen*.

I remember standing in the classroom in Wandsworth one day, looking at this timeline that I had drawn in a black marker on the whiteboard. The *line* represented *time*, and indeed the two words are clearly connected by the phonetic pair *m-n* and a pair of letters that look alike, *l-t* (*t* is an *l* with a line drawn through it). I had marked the different points in time that more or less define our existence – present, past and future – with crosses, and yet the line continued before the past and into the future. It didn't stop where I had drawn the tenses. That is, life exists on earth before and after we arrive here.

But there was something else – all this white space around the line, and even underneath it. I realized that time can only exist inside this white space, otherwise where am I going to be able to draw it? And the white space represents eternity. So time is in eternity, and you will see that this is indeed true if you remember the phonetic pair *m-n*. The word *time* is found inside *eternity* (addition of *r*, the other letters are repeated). Time can only exist because eternity exists, otherwise there is nowhere to put it. In the same way, a line is actually a circle in profile.

Let us look at the word *time*, an extremely important word, I think, and see what else we can find. Well, the obvious thing is that *time* is made up of a cross, *†*, *I* and *me*. So it seems to confirm what I have been saying, that time – our life on this earth – exists in order for us to learn to count down from I to O, to deny ourselves, to lose our life in order to find it in eternity.

Another two words that can be found in *time* are *meet* and *deny*. For the first, we simply allow fluidity to the vowels (*e-i*, the front vowels). For the second, we apply the phonetic pairs *d-t* and *m-n* (remembering that *y* corresponds to *i*). *Meet* and *deny*. I would suggest that *time* is our opportunity to *meet* Christ or to *deny* him. And this meeting will be very important, as we shall see in a moment.

Another word that is clearly related to *time* is *sin* (phonetic pair *m-n*, a step in the alphabet, *s-t*, addition of *e*). We all sin in time. There is no one on this earth apart from Christ who by nature is without sin. In Greek, the word for 'sin', *hamartia*, means 'miss the mark' (and indeed *sin* reads *miss* in reverse). When we sin, we are missing the mark. I don't think we need to punish ourselves all the time, as we frequently do. God is a God of love, he wants to help us on the way, not to punish us. We need to see that we are missing the mark and reorient our lives, which is the meaning of the word for 'repentance' in Greek, *metanoia*, a change of mind, a change of standpoint. We begin to see things in a new light.

Time also has *myth* in it, in reverse (*y* corresponds to *i*, addition of *h/e*). Shakespeare did say, 'All the world's a stage,' while the Spanish playwright Calderón de la Barca says that 'life is a dream' (see the connections between *earth* and *theatre, dream* and *matter*). I think that *time* is somehow a *myth*, and one day it will fizzle out, like a soft drink, to reveal what is underneath (and what was surrounding us, infusing us, all the time).

Christ entered time, he became human, in order to translate for us the meaning of life. We were lost, in need of guidance. God was unknown to us. In fact, up until that point, all we had were precisely myths in order to explain God (or the gods), the different facets of existence, as far as we could understand them.

All through the Gospels, Christ uses parables to teach us. A parable is purportedly a story about someone else that happens outside of time – they are not historical events. This means they are timeless and can refer to us. We have seen the examples of the Parables of the Sower, of the Tares, and of the Workers in the Vineyard. We are the ones who have to hear the word of the kingdom in order to bear fruit. We are the ones who are hired to work in the vineyard. It doesn't matter how much of the day we work, as long as we wish to be hired. We are the ones who must help our brother or sister in need in the Parable of the Good Samaritan.

If we remember the phonetic pair *b-p* (and please note that all the word connections I make are always based on the same fixed rules pertaining to phonetics, the alphabet and the letters' appearance), we will see that *parable* is connected to *Braille*. It is a form of writing for the blind – the spiritually blind, in this case.

So Christ came to translate for us. Christ is the Son of God, this makes him an author. In order to translate, he became human, because translation is human existence per se. Things do not begin with us. Life existed on the earth before we came into existence, and it will continue to exist after we die. Our existence on this earth is limited by time. In fact, we can see that *time* contains *die* (phonetic pair *d-t*, addition of *m*) and *live* (two steps in the alphabet, *l-m* and *t-v*). But we wish to make out we are authors, we draw lines that separate us and lead to conflict. We exalt the author and undervalue the translator enormously (a translation is second-rate, not as good as the original). We fail to realize that things pass through us – the only thing that belongs to us, that we have control over, is our reaction, whether we react with love or hatred, and it is this reaction that will dictate our destiny.

In the act of translation, when we take a text written in one language and write it in another, it is the text that passes through us. All the work we do beforehand – learning the language we are going to translate from, reading the text, looking up words in the dictionary, consulting the author or an expert in their work when we have doubts – is horizontal. It occurs over time. But the act of translation itself, for me, is vertical. It occurs outside time. We catch a current and we ride that current while we are translating. So while all the preparatory work is like an inhalation – we breathe in – the act of translation itself is like an exhalation – we breathe out. One long outbreath. If we are translating an extensive novel, we have to breathe out, to maintain the tension, over quite a lengthy period of time, perhaps months. Obviously, during this time, we are breathing normally (I hope), eating and sleeping. But the act of translation continues, the outbreath doesn't stop, until we reach the end of the text.

This process can be compared to life, in which we are also writing a text, the kind of life we lead, the kind of person we want to be. How the text ends is up to us, but we are always approaching that final sentence, which is like a mooring ring. At this point, our boat, the boat we are travelling on, will nudge up against the wall of the harbour, and we will have arrived.

And where does the text go before it reappears in another language? It exists only in the mind of the translator. That is, for a moment it disappears, it is nowhere to be seen. It has left the source language, but not yet reached the target language. And it is the translator who then writes the text in another language, a truly magical process.

I would like to finish this book by suggesting that Christ came down to earth not only to *translate for us* the meaning of life through parables, but also to *translate us* at our death. We are words in the making. We saw in the first lesson how the elements of speech and creation are breath, water and flesh. Our **breath** leaves our body when we die. Our **flesh** is the body we leave behind, with which we will be reunited at the universal resurrection. And **water** is the water of baptism, the combination of Christ (O_2) and the Holy Spirit (H). These three elements make up speech and enable us to be spoken.

It is Christ who will speak us. He is the Word, after all. It is he who will define us, who will choose the word that best defines us, and speak us into eternity. This is why we must believe in him with every ounce of strength in our bodies, with every straining of our mind. We must believe in him, we must confess him with our breath, we must receive this 'spring of water gushing up to eternal life' in the water of baptism. We must partake of him in the bread of communion. See how close *bread* and *water* are (phonetic pairs *d-t* and *b-w*).

And once we have been spoken into eternity, we will no longer be limited by time.

This is why *eternal* spells *I am free* (phonetic pair *m-n*, pairs of letters that look alike *i-l* and *f-t*).

And once we have been spoken and left God's mouth, we will be able to see him face to face. This is why *eternal* also spells *father* and *I* (a step in the alphabet, *e-f*, pairs of letters that look alike *h-n* and *i-l*). We will have escaped the constraints of the timeline, we will have alighted at our stop, we will have disappeared in the mind of the Translator, who will hold us there as long as he deems necessary – we can trust him to do this – before speaking us into eternity.

POSTSCRIPT

Atom

Breath, water and flesh are the elements of speech, of our existence. All through this book, I have spoken about the progression from the A of creation to the I of the Fall (the era we live in) to the O of repentance/recognition (when we breathe life into the line). When we draw a line through the ego, when we delete the I, this gives us A + O, or Alpha and Omega, the name of God in the Book of Revelation. We have seen how this progression is found in the middle conjunction, 'and', if we write it in capital letters: A 'N' D. The reverse of *and* is *DNA* – it is in our DNA to do this, just as a *hu-man* is made to call on God (*hu* being the first word the human apparatus is capable of making, Sanskrit for 'invoke the gods' and the root of our word *God*).

There is one other word I would like to add. It provides a connection with Carlo Rovelli's book *Seven Brief Lessons on Physics*, from which I borrowed the title for this book. And that is *atom*. An atom was traditionally regarded as the smallest particle of matter in existence. Now we have learned to split the atom into its constituent parts: protons, neutrons and electrons. It doesn't matter. We may remember that a long o in Greek is written *w*. This is the letter *omega*, which happens to be a combination of the name of God in Exodus – *AM* – and *ego*.

Well, we can see this progression, with the I deleted, in the word *atom*. There is the A of creation, the I with a line drawn through it, when we turn away from the demands of the ego and acknowledge God, and the two ways of writing O (O/W, except that the Greek letter *w* has been turned upside down).

So again language confirms this progression. Like the environment, it is made up of 'logoi', fragments of the Word. The whole of human existence is encapsulated in the words we use every day, like a fossil. We just have to have eyes to see it.

Sofia, 25 June-5 July 2021

Seven Brief Lessons on Language is Jonathan Dunne's fourth book on language. He has previously published *The DNA of the English Language* (2007), an introduction to word connections; *The Life of a Translator* (2013), which looks at coincidence in translation; and *Stones Of Ithaca* (2019), a study of the relationship between language and the environment, which uses the example of stones from the beaches of the Greek island of Ithaca.

Jonathan is a graduate in Classics from Oxford University. He has translated more than seventy books from the Bulgarian, Catalan, Galician and Spanish languages for publishing houses such as Penguin Random House, New Directions and Shearsman Books. He lives with his family in Sofia and serves as a subdeacon in the Bulgarian Orthodox Church.

For more information, please visit his personal
website: www.stonesofithaca.com

Lightning Source UK Ltd.
Milton Keynes UK
UKHW041446170222
398746UK00005B/46